Instead of Indonesia

Instead of Indonesia

poems by

Sarah Bein

Red Hen Press

LOS ANGELES

Red Hen Press is a division of Valentine Publishing Group

Cover art: "Inner Landscape XI"
by Ilana Bloch, Los Angeles California

Author photograph by Claressinka Anderson

Edited by Kate Gale

Book design by Mark E. Cull

First Edition
ISBN 1-888996-10-2
Library of Congress Catalog Card Number 98-87337

Red Hen Press
Valentine Publishing Group
P.O. Box 902582
Palmdale, CA 93590-2582

for Claressinka—

il y'a rien comme ta lumière dans ce monde.
je n'oublie jamais, nos rêves.
tout.

Contents

Instead of Indonesia

Paper Birds

I had a thought that when you left
my house yesterday you would not return
I placed paper birds around your face
and heard them say goodbye to you
again as they watched you fly away
I wondered if you knew you would not come back
your eyes refused to stray
from what was in front of you
the inevitable spray of yellow line against
grey gravel

Determined I was to lock myself here
to forget the feel of you against me when I breathe
it is you after all this time that I return to
so I am in my womanly struggle to be alone or to settle
only a small amount I am trying to be alone
but there is this vacancy somewhere in the middle
of my body that bleeds out into my open space
Perhaps it is my part to let it bleed
into my hands my hair
until there is no more
and I am unable to turn around watching you drive away

I wake one day differently to notice
myself in the mirror
to discover a way I have of smiling that is mine
a color I have in my lips that is soft
I will pick up my pen and begin to write
creating my life with two bare hands

Created Myself Naked

Although I said goodbye to you late
on Friday
I still created myself naked
crawled beneath you around you
giving you this last piece of myself
almost to leave you with me
almost to leave myself completely

I am not angry
I never want to leave here
this place in the center of my stomach
instead of asking you to look
and to know
I will show you

I create sacred space for myself
with light and color
with flesh I call my own
But all I remember is you and me
here and we are holy

I see you and beg you
to not forget this
to keep these pieces I have given you
in the palms
of your hands
where it is warm and dark
that some of me will seep
into your veins
plant in your heart
the muscle with chambers

Simply To Touch You

I wait for these things
the man-made glory,
the constancy of clock.
For all I remember
is the lack of time we felt
when my hand fit perfectly into yours
for a blinding second.

Gathering Of Lies

There is a gathering
that has no name, no place
but form and shape
and breath
As a unit it is circle
that has many exits
which you, the participant
in this game
cannot see

There is always a girl there
who is a whore
who is a mother
strings of infant males follow her
like ornaments, brass ones
And they do this dance
and they pretend many things

There is nothing but the adolescent
gape of voices and the stench
of alcohol, the rotting stench
that draws death dancing
among this ritual fire and chanting
"you are one of us now"

And smiling through bruised teeth
and a deformed, ugly mouth
We are all liars,
we who believe
in this sacred ritual,
this mating game
this feeding

I ask is this what you want?
you lift me above your head
and slowly begin to move,
so you can no longer hear me
You are young, you boy, you man
who I have thought better of
I am too much for your hands
my colors have not washed into you
as I had planned,
snake goddess that I am
So you wrap me in lies
and in tissue made of corduroy
and flannel shirts
and command me to dance this dance
and begin to spin for you

I cry like lemonade
once there was no one in this world
except the ocean and the sand
Now there is no exit
and you are no destination

I have myself
my dance, my hair
mine
You sit and poke holes at
this facade which is not a facade
and I wonder where my anger comes from

The color I am is red
perhaps
they can only tear me down
slightly
so you say "I love you"
and I return this gift quietly

and your mouth is in mine
and my stomach churns

Throw wood on this fire
so that you, holy boy,
can see the woman behind the smoke
turn and walk away
realize she was only
temporary anyway

You Are Not The Moon

I am always moving towards
the smell
of your clothes

Your eyes crescent slits
against my shoulder
here I go spinning lies through my teeth
because who am I
to claim you

You are not the moon I am
Those days and nights have disappeared
into nothing
in fact they were nothing
we are nothing
except fourteen days of make-believe
and lust

For Travis

I cannot create you as
a vision of myself
mold you to understand every breath
noise, turn
You said, I cannot
read your mind
and I curled into myself
like a snake ready to strike you
to draw your blood. To have you
inside of me

You said I like
holding your fingers between mine
and feeling your rings press
against my skin
your warm, moist skin
you tell your brother I am a writer who
wears big rings, a woman
who has made you hers

I have met your brothers, lived
in your house
slept in your room
where you see yourself as the tortured martyr
crucified for what you love

Then, do I crucify you?
is that your fear,
ancient and hardened man

You have calloused feet like an Indian
like an old woman
who sells shawls of lima beans
on a hot concrete porch—
who weaves anklets

who weaves her life in to them
I want to wear something you have made

We speak easily when I press
myself against you
and talk to your lips
when I press my lips to yours
my arms around your neck
we become something sacred

You speak to me with perfect stares
open, free
and I smile as my eyes tilt down
watching to see what my hands
will do
if they will encircle yours or stay
as part of my thighs
as part of my body

You will travel the lengths of yourself, soon—
after my many moons
have captured me,
have taken me away
I want to whisper to you
please remember me
one day that was perfect and lay
open in our arms, unwashed
remember that, only
the sun in my hair

That there were many things I
wanted to give to you
so much pressed between
one hour and the next
my world and yours

Once I could not tell
the difference between your body
and mine

Once tears came hot and fast at the thought
of you not understanding
of driving away without looking back—
without noticing I had come to the door
bearing gifts, irises in my hair
a jewel in my stomach

I hold your hand
curl your fingers up around my waist
I walk as you walk
we become my house, my backyard
the air around us rising

Standing under a yellow street light
with my hands in your pockets
and you smiling after me
I could be her
the thing itself, raw and
pure

Yet the paths of our destiny
seem torn and weather beaten
like the face of a cliff, the hollow
of a shell
you realize the intention of my offering
the unselfish wanting
you believe I stand alone
amongst a pool of women
you have already swam through

Is that what you are waiting for?
Me to unveil myself and wish to devour you
like a lioness, make you
nurse me like a cub
I am not dangerous
I do not wear masks
I am safe

I will leave this as something simple
as it was so long ago
can we take that road back, to where
we began this
although we began in fear of one another
let that be healed
let us learn to trust
and leave it at this

I am a woman who wears very large rings
who wishes to bring to you,
some new part of herself

You have shown me that I am universal
that we are universal
and so I see you in my house
in my room, in the mountains
of which I was borne
you wash up on my beach
and I cradle you
wipe the sand and the tide
from your hair, my hair

We see that nothing exists in isolation,
and so as long as I am—
I find nowhere you are not

Journey

Where you come from
there is no ocean
no bed
sod and rock

You are alone
among the carcass of fish and brine
you begin to crawl
a rasp in your stomach takes you deeper
where you hear your blood
swishing your muscles straining

The journey to water and sky
the beginning of salt
you have found this place
underneath yourself
that is no longer life, no longer death
but the synapse between

Every possibility every exit
remains in this field
somewhere between long grains
You see them you even
acknowledge them
but you continue
through yourself and your mother
by the fire
knitting a purple sweater
her son will never wear because he is dead

You think you are male
but are no longer sure
where? where was it?
behind the field of your life
at the beginning of your death

when you had a name
and a place
and someone
who loved you

You find yourself
on the underside of the moon
among craters and waterless oceans
and begin to hike deep streams and fields
like the one you had just crawled out of
Something inside you continues to search
through the bodies of dead whales
the hollowed-out bones of the elephants

Suddenly you forget your purpose your name
among clouds of grey and the smell
of raw rotting flesh.
But now you distinctly feel your maleness
like a mass of strength among the other debris
rising like hot sewage
The machine of decay is alive
you can see his eyes
and they are somehow the eyes of your father
the generic empty male eyes

You have yourself in your hands
your identity and purpose here
in this field in this glass tube
your voice (which has suddenly appeared)
echoes and rises into this black atmosphere
of styrofoam and bones
You are aware you are naked
yet you go on unaware
of light and of breath
driven by the mechanic pulse in your legs

If you go further somehow you know
you will make a choice
it is only this awareness of choice you feel
All else has been left to the machine
to the living suction of your life
Your consciousness remains confused
An idea to go back? to go on?
You feel hands pull
the need to stop—
for an end to this confusion

You want to have a bed to have an ocean
to be in love
but you are a man and men cannot love
so you go on into the next field
which is violet and lavender
You feel warmth here the need to bathe
to cease this meandering walk this quest
There are curves here you are not aware of
curves like hips like breasts like thick thighs

You feel awkward
Are you naked? You feel eyes gaze into you
or the collective pressure of one single eye
either way you are alien
You must leave this curvy forest
which is soft and warm
something is not right

So you pick up a single lavender stone
and notice you no longer have eyes
you no longer are a body a face
but a single mass of non-conscious thought
This is okay because something tells you
you must go on

You have further feats
more fields to conquer
perhaps you are the machine,
perhaps you are the carcass of a male
or a fish

Julie

This is the day of your funeral
when my hands pressed tightly
against my hair and remembered
your hair the curls of wheat
the smell of your house
like bread rising

There is nothing to say
nothing except that you had life
and you were love itself
not the meaning but the thing
the nakedness the simplicity

Yet this is how I remember you
smiling in your mother's arms
playing the piano
To live that last day with you
after five years I would take you into my room
into the violet light of childhood
and whisper fears and powdery white pills
to death

Julie I was sure you would survive
get out
of this mother's cage
this anger over girlish failures
were you more than I was able to see
selfish woman I am
who remembers only the anniversary of your death
the raised veins in your hands
protecting your skin

I remember the way you would cry
lean over to me
whispering secrets
we became holy
I don't remember ever telling you
I loved you
While I lost you and you
lost yourself daily
And so when I saw your mother driving beside me
the Tuesday after your death
gripping the steering wheel
convulsing like a mad woman
there was nothing for me
to do but turn away and drive

And so driving I took you with me
now this feeling just below my heart
I collect pieces of you from myself
and place them together
that is my part
I light candles and lie in warm water
that is my part
and it is enough
it is more than enough

Loose Change

love is
worth nothing until it has been tested
by its own defeat

—Adele Ne Jame

I have come from raking in the yard
Saturday lays quiet in my hands
I have been raking something temporary
like us
There is no proof except a gum wrapper
left on your floor
so you crunch it in your hand
carry this with you
in your pocket
next to loose change
the receipt for your stereo
or the night we went to dinner
and your keys
This is how I will remember you
we moved on into this unlabeled world
untouched and clean
as singular travelers
through this mute land

Pink Beginnings

knowing nothing can save us
from what hourly we are making or unmaking—
—Adele Ne Jame

Driving in a car
through the Northeastern landscape
reminding me of whispers
and an end to a foreseeable journey
we looked down into canyon and sea
felt something pink beginning
amongst us

We remember the hum
of an air conditioner
the smell of carpet
raw and thick
so unlike the outside our window
soft dew ripening needles of grass
the feeling that we here
3000 miles East
were lost

That is why after these years
we were able to move on
to be found to find
Past the New England real estate and
blue-collar towns
into the familiar landscape of soil
and water
we sat and with our hands naked in clay
began to create
knowing the difference between us
trying to translate images sensations
lifetimes into language something tangible
and common so that
we can begin to forgive and to make

A Garden To Fly Over

—For Kate

You plant tomatoes and peppers
in your garden to feel your life
beginning there
with long legs in a beige gown
you outstretch your arms and breathe
for this one day that is yours

This is how you have learned to live
pressing your lips against the seconds
of a clock cupping your hands around an hour
and the movement of the sun
this circle has become your life
to plant to breathe eat sleep

Daily you live as watercolor
melting and becoming
at night under stars ticking
reflecting pearls of leaves and arms of trees
you watch vegetables grow
and with them you dance this dance
of offering and resurrection

With the children around you
and the divinity of little girls
whispering and giggling like soft bubbles
you imagine these things in your garden
you imagine a winged horse and a lover
flying over your house and into your bed
you do not need rescuing
only proof that your world exists

Your books become your children
and your lovers around you
as if your words written smoothly
have become your armor
so that you are safe to dance
to paint mountains and oceans which
are yours to fly over
feeling the colors seep between your fingers
crawl underneath your nails into your skin

You go on to plant oranges and apples avocados
you have stood naked in the rain in Guatemala
with Mark the one you say you will marry
whose hair you take in your hands
whose soft body you hold
with whom you share your life
this garden of your life

Your children at your knees
you hike
into Amazon and water to take this garden
further into acres of vegetation and soil
to discover more
to write stories of Spanish women
women who spend lifetimes planting and watering
so your pen is moved magically in
your right hand across acres of paper
and you continue to breathe

Upon your return you lie in bed
for weeks ill with fever
perhaps you had seen too much
a life without weeds or worms
and you could not go on writing this
but your life began a collection of delusions
on paper because you could not stop
writing or painting

You have wiped salt from your skin
remembering the old woman
who took you in her hands and whispered to you
like you whisper to Mark
like you whisper to your children
telling them stories you are
telling yourself

A World Without Voices

Lopez discovered the Blue Mound people
in the desert
born without vocal cords
he began books of them
anatomically human as we see humans
yet without the hollow muscle of their throat
giving their existence shape and sound
so they created life without sound
they did not notice this absence
they created their limbs
began to dance with the desert
people created from the sand molded into dirt
for years he excavated and watched their remains
worshipping their bones and dust
something like O'Keeffe would have done
spiraling color on paper into texture
and human skin
something like a miracle
instead they took the living soil
from underneath themselves
created mounds of blue alkaline mist
he does not know if they breathed
how they communicated
perhaps that is what we are searching for
a world without voices
a man and a woman together in a room
perhaps naked and single
holding in their hands something like a painting
or a perfect blue circle

Flowers And Bones

—For G.O'Keeffe

You took this color of red blue pink
as it was in the ground single and whole
and you melted them together
into the texture of the sky
leaving us no explanation
only the imagined feel of your fingers

There is no presence of light
here in your world
only skin and bone
pulsing through canvas
you leave us in the space
between ourselves
to close our eyes
and lean backwards in the wind
to lose fear of falling or losing

You were an old woman who saw color
becoming flowers
your painting languid and large
they move like water they flow and they tide
creating Gods and monsters of all of us
you are Michelangelo in his vision
of a goddess trapped within a
solitary block of stone
Go woman artist and free her

You free us all and we become you
a single piece of you
a bleed of pink a soft curve of a woman's body
you saw and painted
to live alone in the desert
with a man and paintbrushes
to imagine walls of cave and stone
covered in these woman-flowers
skulls of life and humans
where you sat clothed in black
and began amongst darkness
and then brilliantly,
were borne into light

You Never Could

Like a dream you came to me early
I still held fresh globes of sleep in my hands
the world around my bed hung thick, moist.
You said, "I thought you could make us coffee."
Hours later I just want to go back to
answering the phone, to opening the door.
To your bright face six in the morning leaning against mine.
Help me, I have not woken from sleep. I was an imposter.
Was today with you? I am on the planet of last night.

Now that I am leaving Friday, do you drive past
my window? And what has happened
to this great lost love of ours.
How do I learn to reconcile the past within me
while there still exists your smiling face?

And Oh, this one great . . . fading.

I have but a ring on my finger from the sea
you gave me, an inlay pearl I liked in August
you gave me in January. How do I learn
to hold these six months somewhere warm and safe?
Somewhere I wanted you to be.

And I am angry with you for showing up at my doorstep,
angry with you for making me fall in love with this
non-existent you, for removing yourself just so much,
for moving and moving and removing.

Angry with you for the angel you were this morning,
for knowing too much, for seeing through.

And it's not fair that you woke me this morning
and it's not fair that you entered my life
carrying a book, a pen, a camera, flowers.

That you met me because you liked my poetry
loved me because you wanted to know,
lost me because you never could.

I see how easy it would be to slip into you,
ships passing in a harbor, exchanging paint, residue,
inflicting bruises, chipping paint, moving on.

But you didn't wake me.
This was the one morning I lay in bed until five
playing over the goodbye, how to mean it,
how to say good luck with everything and walk away.
You were the intruder I always wanted,
taking and taking and then . . .

And it's not fair that we were left
with a choice, both of us leaving,
you not coming with me, me uncertain I wanted you to.

That you met me because you liked my poetry
loved me because you wanted to know
lost me because you never could.

A Land Between Goodbyes

I am liquid before poured carefully into its pitcher
I think it would be nice to stay here for a while
raw and shapeless in sheets

thoughts come like dust
the purpose of this morning is to lie here

These were not my hands or my clothes
they belonged to my December self
the one who saw you whole within a wrapper of ice
and decided to hold your hand

Orchid In Plastic

Waking and holding Wednesday in my hands
for a fleeting second
before evening came
And this becomes all
the moon succeeding the sun and the lapse
in between which is terror

It was not until you brought me
an orchid in a box
that I began to shake
perhaps because that orchid could not breathe
or begin to breathe in its plastic wrapping
Perhaps it is just that I understand
exactly
how that is

Infection

Hours after
I am in a bed with sheets.
My thighs ache,
my insides burn.
I have an infection that began
last night with you rushing
into me,
telling me over and over, that
you were real.

Today I try to wash my hands,
but they are red. My body is red.
I am raw, and I reach
in between myself to take back
what I cannot.

My Mistake

I think I miss you. You become
a part of myself that I carry
always, like a fold in my skirt.
I sail my boat towards yours, and wonder
what will become
of us. I no longer
climb you like a mountain,
become you like color.

No, only have stood back from the canvas
of my life to find
your unmistaken handprint.

The Place Where I Began

The on-ramp to your freeway was closed, so
I took a detour to get to your house.
I drove past orange yellow cliffs jutting out
into the light of dusk when the clouds are full.
The air pink hung about my hair like wet sheets.

We walked through dirt, me in your
brother's old shoes, through the canvas
of what was beginning and ending. It was
still light out and we held hands, briefly.
Your eyes so like a little boys, still moving
up my body. You saw my doubts heavy
and wet like laundry which will not dry despite
a persistent wind. You, like the wind, said—

What will this be like *after*,
as if this word took on shape and form.
After you are a grown up.
After you become a need inside which will not stop.
I'll say I am ready for this
and you'll reach into me, curling
your body around mine and drawing circles
on my back with your fingertips.

It was in your backyard hours later, when there was
no sun, where we placed the possibility of an end
high above our heads and said, look—
There is a world of what's right. There.
And we looked. We saw the burden of time, all
we could discern was the man-made end like a road block.

So I threw my arms around you, crying into
your hair, burying my fingers in your skin
telling you how sorry I was. I left
your house before unpacking my dreams for us.
Before allowing you to wear me like a glove,
drove home through night thick mists.
No longer able to see canyon or stars, night or day.
Just the world I left behind and the one I will enter.

I am in traffic, just give me one moment
to find my way back home.

In that hour people lost their faces
and became one unmistakable image, I am a traveller.
You said, this was not love at first sight after all
and then I knew you were right, you could never
have me with logic like that, like a two year old boy.
So I am home unpacking our entire relationship

like shredding old layers of skin. The pink
dress I would have worn tonight, the things I was
going to whisper in bed.
I place them in drawers and cabinets.
I place them inside myself where they belong.

You held me like warm bread and whispered delusions
of yourself in my ear through morning.

But your own road was blocked by something
obtrusive and strange, and the detour I took
to come to you led me back to where I began.

Ah, Girl

You are in a room surrounded by ocean.
You hear rough tide gulling at the window.
You sit with your legs
up close to you, speaking with a man in a
voice so familiar to him.

Laugh, speak louder, show me your tricks.

You want to give him everything. All you are—
but he cannot have it. Your words are water. They
hit the concrete of his head.
You want to lay yourself down by him
every night, no longer by the sea or air.
Your skin shrinks,

it cannot breathe. You stopped the in and out
motion that, would just come.
Now it is cold out and you are left
with his body against yours.

And that is all you are.
A place for him to sleep.

Red Like My Dreams

I wish you could see what I see
I wish that was your car parked outside my window
I wish this was your sweater I wear
that you could feel me when I was not around

When you look in the mirror
see my face
remember my place in your pool of a life
somewhere between hills and wind
Somewhere where colors are black and orange
red
like my dreams

Something like New Mexico or my dream
where we stood together over the folds
of the Grand Canyon You looked at my face and whispered
this is where I was born—

and in that second I knew your life
like my own hands Knew you like the feel of my
clothes against my skin warm and becoming
You becoming a notion of comfort

So now I am awake still dreaming
of an opening until the next of lives
where we will begin as we have before, when the
world is violet amongst each other
like stars red ones which exploded into light

You Will Return Again And I Will Wait For You

You are on a ship sailing to Berlin
from there to Helsinki, St. Petersburg,
Stockholm— While I am thinking
of your hands in mine, you are watching
the ocean chop against steel and wood.

I have done all I could.
I have written to you in Innsbrch, the town
you were a boy in, living in your own
apartment at age fifteen. I wish I had
known you then, the feel of your hair.

But who am I when there are lifetimes
I do not know about you. Adventures and women
when I was nothing but a distant thought
hammering the corner of your mind, before
I had materialized into the woman who stood before you
at three in the morning, watching you smoke
your cigarette and say goodbye to the ocean
for a day, say goodbye to me.

So now that I am real I want to be with you
as you see everything for the fifth time
things I have never seen
things that reach inside and touch me like
never before, like the way I wanted for you.
But the obstacle of time kneaded its fingers
into our heads, pressing into us the unmistakable
feeling of doubt.

July sixteenth you will return like a small boy
living alone again moving from one woman
to the next. Not bothering with
love, money, regret—
only this notion of yourself as apart from others,
this notion I was born with.
That we are autonomous.

Then to Paris, the city of which I live.
New York, where America is tolerable.
I could have gone on
wondering, would it have been possible,
to leave this world and enter the next
with you.

What Really Happened

After she gave her eyes to him
he could not see.
He could not
filter so much
energy and light,
such alive things.

So they lived their lives
like trees
alone.

Midnight In London

I miss you, your smile
when, for a second,
you look directly into my eyes
and we appear the same.
Your awkward hands
which cannot decide
whether to touch my body
or yours.
Your mouth which speaks truth and
forces me into silence.

Her Red Round Room

This isn't my room she thinks
these are not my hands
          music, she hears music instead of the pulse of the
room
          instead of her breath pulsing   inout   inout

She wears pink always when she sees him
she wears pink.
          Part of the   ritual
          Part of the   game
see, I know what I am doing, exactly.

Always the scenes of her life open with a woman waiting
on a bed   the muffling of a car   footsteps to the window
wait, is he here? nonono

see, I have control over my language   you are a silly boy

But— (even when he is in the room)
               something is different

"hello". . . . . . "hello". . . . . (sit with me)
Hands
Skin . . . breath
Silk, you feel like silk   and
          oh baby with your pretty
                                        face.
bones legs a pink jewel in her stomach the salt
          of your lips

Movement   new scene
Action.
—.
—.

She wants to take him for a walk—around her,
curl him into her   but slowly now
        fairy dust   glitter
Baby you are . . .

Back in the swirl of her red round bed, the river
flowing out of her   her water reaching him wanting
        nothing   other than this. Here.

It is as if he . . . came
                                        from
                                                her
lavishly from between her legs.   But—

The melting smell of vanilla and a candle burning
        . . . with your pretty face . . .

He says, cook me pasta   dance for me   spin me inside
        inside she smiles
she the exhibition he,   he the stage.   And oh baby

  the way you move.

Back in the circle of her room she says I want to . . . you
I want to paint you, do not move   sit here
                I want to . . .

And he cannot speak and he does not speak, and then . . .

Movement   a departure   fading music

she walks toward him slowly like an

animal she
curls the air forming the
language of her life with her hands

. . . . . understand me
see me
speak to me.   there . . . and ooh . . .

(as if she is translatable (to him))

she is waiting for the one who . . .
but for now
he sits in a chair
she . . . him   she straddles him
(oh baby)

she moves silently until she is done
he calls   her name

she rises   repeatedly   from oceans
she sucks   him   into her
and then . . . she . . . him

a silent   slow

fading

Once In Catalina, I Could Not Stop This

When the water washes against me
I come back to your memory
You see a woman in white on a beach
you see her hands
          like gloves covering
You cannot feel her turning away from you
but you wonder

(her hands like sea mist)

the single spray of the ocean
her life of overlapping currents
pulling every direction
you cannot feel her
She is somewhere
you can't see
You like her bottom lip how it
curls inward like a sea snail as
She walks
          away

Where You Are There Is No Light

He might have thought she was
no longer there
if it had not been for the glint
of her body in the darkness.
—Gabriel Garcia Marquez

Before her, you never thought about
what would come next, after.
Before her, you never thought you could belong
to anyone but yourself
(a small unrelenting feeling
        under the bones of your ribcage).
She stays somewhere close, you hear her even
when you don't want to—the feeling grows.

Although there were others you allowed to pass through
you, it was only that, a night of scotch,
the bed sheets, wet. When you remember, you see the
scent of their hair, rising around you like she did.
In my head, a part of me is always journeying toward you,
an ocean of skin, a breath of stars.

You will not be a destination.

She is something you keep coming back to
like rain in August.
You try to close your eyes
        but won't,
destroy your hands
        but can't.

She is rain in August. I haven't slept for days.

You search for an ending that will not come
not yet, you think, not yet
and move across the stage
to where there is no light.

A Bath Of Perfect Light—Drowning

She wants an exit a prison
a last good-
                              bye
But he is beautiful and without
speaking to him she said forever
she said now
Last night she dreamed (as she does)
the number six—not the thought
but the thing itself raw and twisting
in her mind nothing was
concrete any longer so she decided to run
hard and fast
to spin somewhere
around herself until

he could not see in
until he could not come in
until he could not have her with the word
"love" alone She looks for his eyes
in her dreams cannot find them
cannot find anything but
a kind of softness in the middle
of her life growing unfamiliar
and dark

In her sleep she sees hands reaching
the light she is covered in
perfect and she sees him—
like an ending to something that
was never begun

Instead Of Indonesia

Paul-Il n'est pas permis de resumer une vie riche,
creatrice, en si peu de termes.

Before the napping
a pear wind blowing the blue window open
pushing at the silks on the bed Last night
the cooking of olive
          oil in a pan like the rise of the sea
the peeling of pear the sweetness
of the chutney like the mesh of your
fingers into me
This time you have forgotten the glasses
down the hall so I go get them
I smile when they are blue like the calm of
          your face You pour wine
I tell you this

I brush by you to watch the window in your kitchen
Your words are yellow like the chutney-lime sauce
          over rice
I am your chef you say
          You hand me many knives
I wonder what this means

This morning the elastic of your words
were the frying of mango and rice I wake
to the blue glasses by the outreach of my hair
          I smell you like the night
                    (the chopping and
                              chopping . . .)
feel the mush of the sauce between my ankles
          where your tongue was
The orange night
          (your tongue)

a myth of pear mango both blossoms opening
into something like
the
sea

Where Love Goes

This time, Lola, I let you go.
This time I set us free.
Love is a shadow
How you cry after it
Listen: there are its hooves, it has
gone off like a horse.
—From *The American Woman in the Chinese Hat*

"You're always packing," he says
and I can tell he is   something
we haven't spoken in a while

And I can't find the words to say what I want
          (Be something . . . please)
I remember your words slanted
arched to fit the contours of my hands
          (I will always leave)
I don't have the words to say to you
I don't even know how to begin to ask for them
Instead I hold in my hands
the place we stood
where once we thought
anything
was possible   (nothing was true)

Keeping Her Face

Today I thought I saw her walking by me.
She was carrying strawberries in a brown paper bag,
the juice pressing through.
She was having trouble
keeping the wind out of
her hair, keeping
the hair out of
her face, keeping
her face
covered.

Lime. Mango. Cilantro.

After you,
I touch myself differently,
you rub sensation from my body,
your arms like wiping crumbs from my tablecloth.

(see . . . my hand trembles even as I write)

Last night your ghost moving
across my purple room,
your blue words
        in the green fire sea
(candles dripping down the ceiling)
I love you with the wine sauce
        —something coming on and on—
sometimes the color of you is grey-blue
fall in love with the limes
        your chopping and
                chopping of
                        cilantro.

You moved through me like an intruder
I think pale yellow, sometimes I want you
to be—
        chopping and chopping.
We kiss with mango
        (you are mango)
you squeeze yourself down my breasts
you smile in a flickering orange light

The rice tastes sweet like loneliness,
you have never looked stranger to me.
        Stranger? No.
You dip me in the batter, say,
I love you in these small glasses.

Sometimes the light changes
Lime. Mango. Cilantro.
(you look like rice)
In the hollow of your stomach where there is no food
(you look like loneliness)

Sometimes when I cry the tears are the wine sauce
I cry your chopped cilantro,
your steamed mango,
your twisted
lime.

Nothing Can Save This

I can reach deep like digging through dirt
          for my blindness
I show it to you . . . say
look this is what I have done
This
And I can remember the years with you
and your answers clear and
right like the rain.

You questioned the time it took to begin writing
          my hair wet from your storms
this time you have no answer

you showed me a place in the ground
"where I can bury blindness" you say
          you carry with you a shovel a canteen of water
"this is as good a place as any"

you begin your right walk and away   we will run

and my hands will follow
with paper

and pencils

This Is What Happened

He said, I love you more than London
and she gave her eyes to him
she gave everything to him.

Biographical Note

Sarah Bein lives in New York City. *Instead of Inodonesia* and her first book of poetry, *This Quiet Sun* (Red Hen Press, 1996), were written before she was eighteen. *This Quiet Sun* has been used as text at various colleges and universities including Boston University. She continues to write poetry, and she attends college in New York.